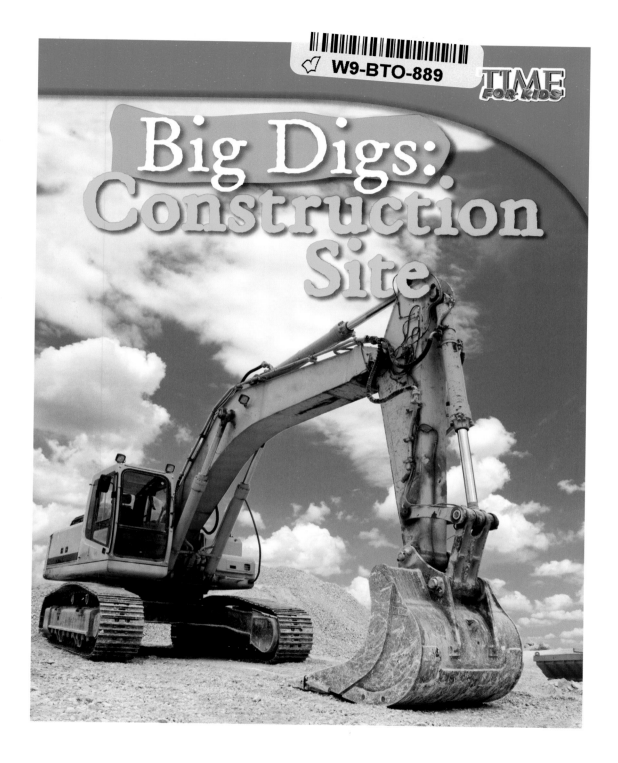

Big Digs: Construction Site

TIME FOR KIDS!

Lisa Greathouse

Consultant

Timothy Rasinski, Ph.D.
Kent State University

Publishing Credits

Dona Herweck Rice, *Editor-in-Chief*

Robin Erickson, *Production Director*

Lee Aucoin, *Creative Director*

Conni Medina, M.A.Ed., *Editorial Director*

Jamey Acosta, *Editor*

Heidi Kellenberger, *Editor*

Lexa Hoang, *Designer*

Stephanie Reid, *Photo Editor*

Rachelle Cracchiolo, M.S.Ed., *Publisher*

Teacher Created Materials

5301 Oceanus Drive
Huntington Beach, CA 92649-1030
http://www.tcmpub.com

ISBN 978-1-4333-3662-1

© 2012 Teacher Created Materials, Inc.
Reprinted 2013

Table of Contents

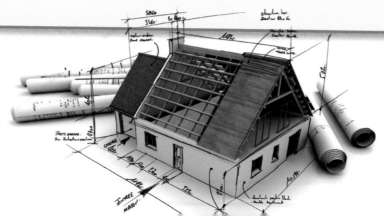

A Visit to a Construction Site

Put on your hard hat! We are going to visit a construction site. The construction crew is getting ready to build a house. But the planning began long before they arrived.

The Architect

The process begins with an **architect**. This is a person who designs houses. Architects also design other structures such as skyscrapers and bridges. Architects

do more than plan what a house looks like. They want the houses they design to be safe to live in. And they want them to be strong enough to last a very long time.

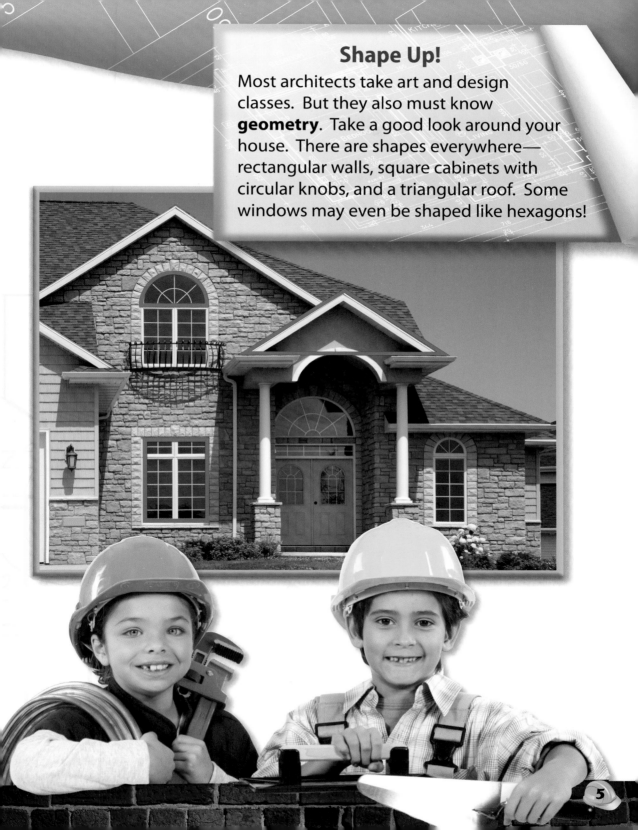

Shape Up!

Most architects take art and design classes. But they also must know **geometry**. Take a good look around your house. There are shapes everywhere—rectangular walls, square cabinets with circular knobs, and a triangular roof. Some windows may even be shaped like hexagons!

The architect meets with the clients to find out what kind of house they want. How many bedrooms do they need? How many bathrooms? Do they want a big kitchen? How about an attic? Or a pool in the backyard? There are dozens—sometimes hundreds—of decisions to make! Many decisions depend on how many people will be living in the house.

Decisions also depend on the client's **budget**. That is how much money they want to spend.

▼ Construction workers review a blueprint.

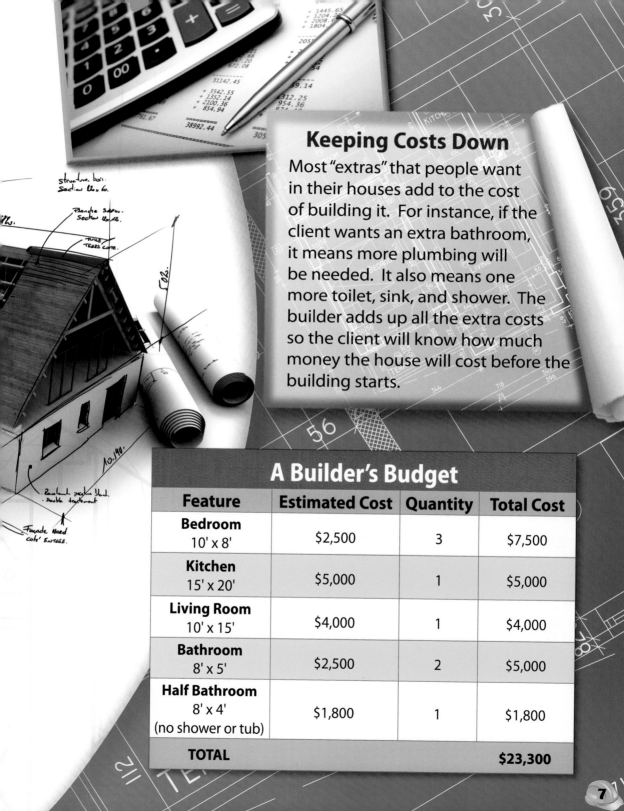

Keeping Costs Down

Most "extras" that people want in their houses add to the cost of building it. For instance, if the client wants an extra bathroom, it means more plumbing will be needed. It also means one more toilet, sink, and shower. The builder adds up all the extra costs so the client will know how much money the house will cost before the building starts.

A Builder's Budget

Feature	Estimated Cost	Quantity	Total Cost
Bedroom 10' x 8'	$2,500	3	$7,500
Kitchen 15' x 20'	$5,000	1	$5,000
Living Room 10' x 15'	$4,000	1	$4,000
Bathroom 8' x 5'	$2,500	2	$5,000
Half Bathroom 8' x 4' (no shower or tub)	$1,800	1	$1,800
TOTAL			**$23,300**

▲ An architect creates a blueprint.

The architect prepares a detailed drawing. This is called a **blueprint**. It shows what the house will look like on the outside and on the inside. It shows everything from the **beams** that hold up the house to how the plumbing will work. Blueprints show measurements for each part of the house. Every wall, door, window, and closet has an exact measurement. One mistake can cause big problems for the builders.

Homes Around the World

Houses come in all shapes and sizes. Different materials are used to build homes in different parts of the world. In Africa, many people live in mud huts. In Mongolia, sheep herders live in *yurts*, or portable folding homes.

▲ a yurt

◄ a mud hut

Why Is a Blueprint Blue?

Blueprints, or building plans, were invented in the 1800s. Plans were drawn on tracing paper. The drawing was placed over paper treated with chemicals. Then it was set under a bright light in a developing solution. The result was blue paper with white lines showing the original plans. No ink was used, so the design could not be smudged or faded. Most architects now create plans on computers. But the term *blueprint* is still used to refer to any detailed plan.

Building the Team

Now it's time for a builder, or **general contractor**, to step in. This is the person who will hire all the people who are needed to build a house.

The team includes a **surveyor** (ser-VEY-er) and **foundation** builders. There are plumbers and **electricians**. There are painters and **landscapers**. It is the general contractor's job to keep everything on schedule so the house is completed on time.

The Building Team

Many people work together to build a house. The general contractor oversees all the workers.

General Contractor

| Surveyors | Foundation Builders | Plumbers | Electricians | Painters | Landscapers |

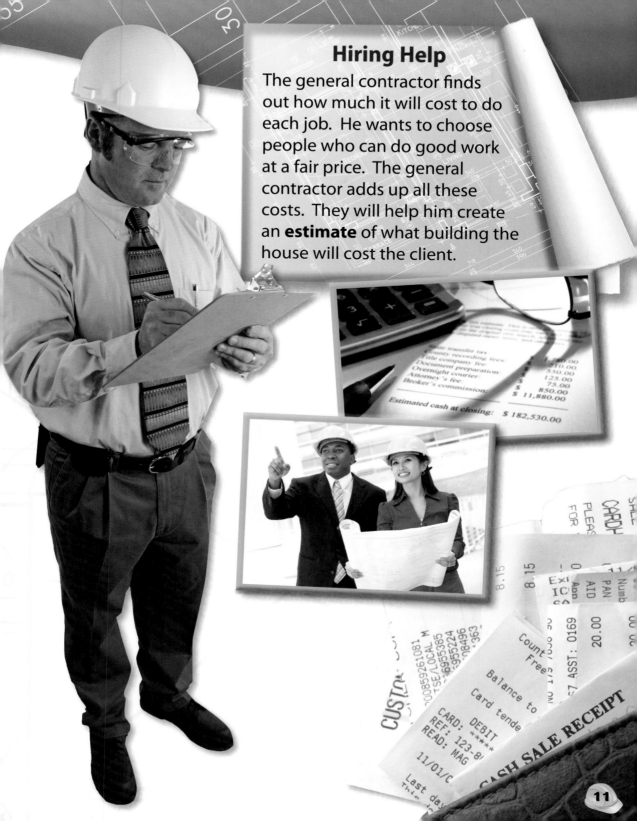

Hiring Help

The general contractor finds out how much it will cost to do each job. He wants to choose people who can do good work at a fair price. The general contractor adds up all these costs. They will help him create an **estimate** of what building the house will cost the client.

One of the first people on the team is the land surveyor. The surveyor maps out where the **property** begins and ends. Wooden stakes are placed to mark exactly where the house will be built.

Land surveying was established as a profession during the Roman Empire. Surveyors use geometry, engineering, mathematics, and physics to do their jobs.

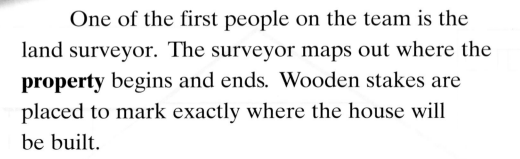
modern surveying equipment ➤

▲ a surveyor at work

Famous Surveyors

George Washington, Thomas Jefferson, Abraham Lincoln, Meriwether Lewis, William Clark, and Daniel Boone were all land surveyors at some point in their lives.

drawings of old surveying tools ▼

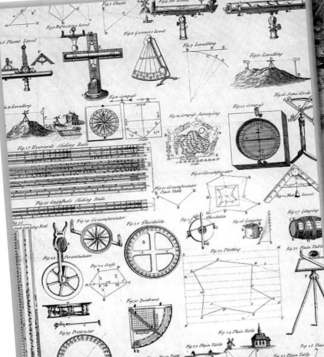

▲ a portrait of George Washington working as a surveyor in Virginia

A Strong Foundation

It's time for a **bulldozer** to clear the land. Workers dig a hole for the foundation of the house. The foundation is one of the most important parts of a house. It supports the weight of the house. That means the foundation must be very strong and last for a long time. Some houses last for hundreds of years!

Many houses are built on a **concrete** slab foundation. First, concrete is poured in trenches around the edges of the foundation. This creates the house **footings**. Now,

▲ Workers smooth the concrete after it is poured in the trenches.

when concrete is poured for the foundation, it will dry in the right shape. If the house has a basement, the foundation will be poured into a hole that is eight feet deep.

The Difference Between Concrete and Cement

Cement is made of ground limestone and clay. It is one of four ingredients that make up concrete. Concrete is a mixture of cement, gravel, sand, and water.

▼ Pouring concrete into the footings takes patience.

◄ The barrel of this truck mixes concrete.

Plumbing Possibilities

Ever wonder what happens when you flush the toilet? The water and waste get sucked down the drain of the toilet. It goes to a city wastewater treatment plant to be cleaned. Or it might go to a **septic tank** under the property.

The plumbing crew connects the pipes from the bathrooms, kitchen, and laundry room. This allows water to come in through the faucets and go out to the right place!

▲ Septic tanks are buried underground.

Did You Know?

An average family of four in the United States uses about 400 gallons of water per day.

Following the Rules

Construction crews have many rules to follow. These are called *building codes*. For instance, plumbers can only use pipes with certain sizes of openings, or **diameters**. The pipes must be placed at specific angles. Plumbers must follow hundreds of pages of codes.

Safety Rules

Construction workers must build safe buildings. They must take care of their own safety as well. Check out this list of safety gear they need to be safe:

- reflective vests
- hard hats
- gloves
- goggles
- steel-toed boots

▲ Being safe requires careful measurements.

Framing the House

Now it's time for the framing crew to step in. They will construct the floor over the foundation. The floor is supported by wooden boards, or **lumber**. Lumber can be cut to many sizes. The lumber that is often used for floors measures 2 inches thick by 10 inches wide. You may also see them called *2-by-10s,* or *2 x 10s.* These boards are then covered with big sheets of **plywood**.

builders laying down a wooden floor

Plant a Tree!

It takes about 27,000 feet of wood to build the average house. That is nearly 100 trees!

Now it is time for the outside walls to go up. The lumber for walls is often 2 inches thick by 4 inches wide and is known as *2-by-4s*. Openings for the doors and windows are measured and cut.

Then it's time to work on the roof. It is very important to have a strong roof that lasts a long time and does not leak.

Roofs used to be built by hand. Today builders often use premade wooden **trusses**. They can be ordered in any size, and they go up fast. The crew makes sure to leave room for the chimney.

Roof Shapes

If you drive around your neighborhood, you may see many different roof shapes. Most roofs are angled. This is so rain can run off the sides and snow will not weigh down a flat surface.

roof trusses ➤

Going Up!

Sometimes, a **crane** is used to lift the trusses and place them on top of the walls. The trusses are tied to the walls with small metal plates. The roof is then covered in plywood and special tar paper. Then the **shingles** are nailed on.

Shingles come in all shapes, sizes, colors, and materials. ➤

The Exterior

So, what should the house look like from the outside? Choices include brick, stone, and **stucco** (STUHK-oh). Some houses are built with vinyl siding. It is made from thin sheets of plastic.

Windows and doors are installed. If measurements are not exact, the owners might wind up with a cold house!

▼ stone

vinyl siding ▲

brick ➤

▲ stucco

Building a Green House

Many builders today are "going green." Here are some ways house construction can be friendlier to the environment.

Material	What It Does
solar panels	Placed on the roof, these use the power from the sun to generate electricity used in the house.
wind turbines	A wind-power system collects energy when the wind blows, turning it into electricity.
low-flow toilets	These use 1.6 gallons per flush instead of 7 gallons.
CFL lightbulbs	Compact fluorescent light (CFL) bulbs use a quarter of the electricity of traditional bulbs.
recycled items	Materials, such as concrete and glass, are used again in new ways.
flooring	Fast-growing cork and bamboo are being used instead of hardwood floors that destroy forests.

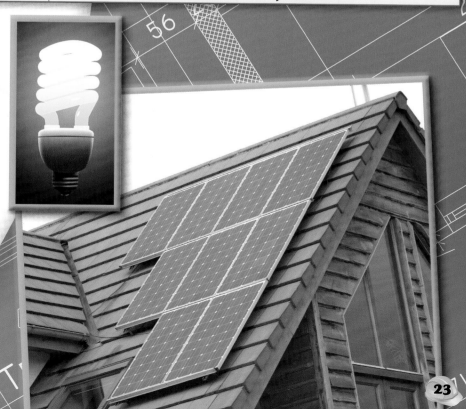

Compact fluorescent lightbulbs are an easy way to "go green" at home. ➤

This roof has solar panels. They generate electricity for the house. ➤

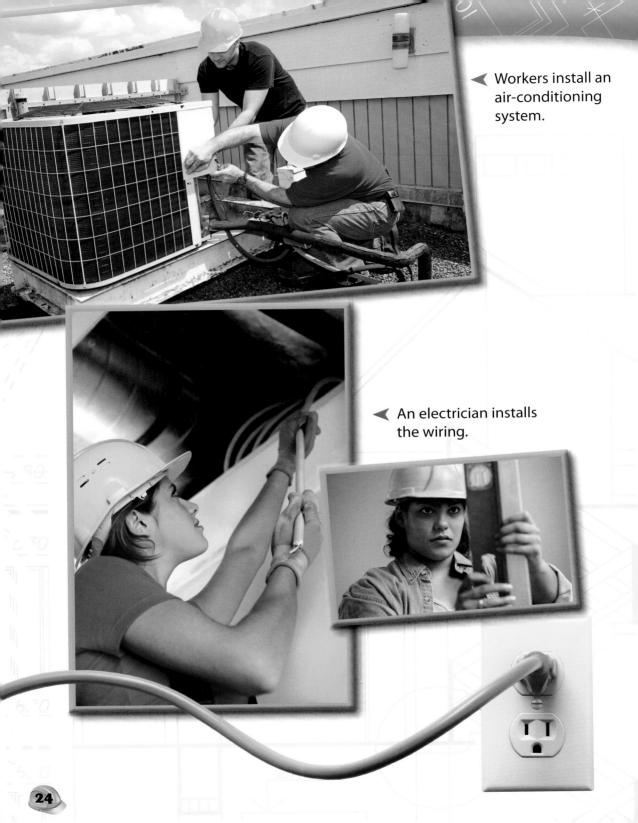

Workers install an air-conditioning system.

An electrician installs the wiring.

Flip the Switch!

Without electricians, we would all be in the dark. They set up a system that safely sends power to all the rooms and **appliances** in the house. Electricians install all the wiring, outlets, switches, and light fixtures.

Another crew installs the furnace and air-conditioning system. This will keep the house cool in the summer and warm in the winter.

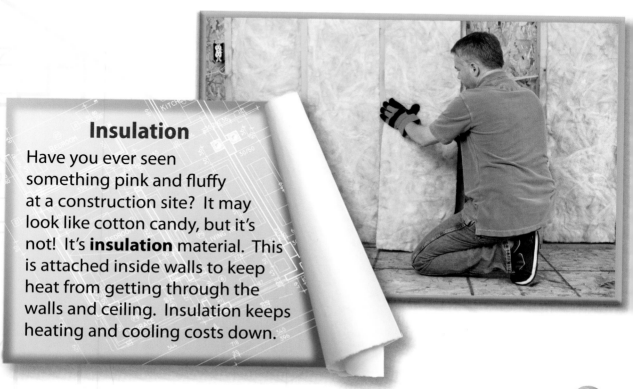

Insulation

Have you ever seen something pink and fluffy at a construction site? It may look like cotton candy, but it's not! It's **insulation** material. This is attached inside walls to keep heat from getting through the walls and ceiling. Insulation keeps heating and cooling costs down.

Finishing Touches

The house may look almost complete from the outside. But on the inside, it still looks like a construction site until the **drywall** goes up. These are wide, flat boards that cover the walls. After you sand them down, it's time to paint. Each room can have its own color.

Then carpet, tile, or other types of flooring are laid down. Kitchen and bathroom cabinets are installed. So are countertops, toilets, sinks, and showers. Appliances, such as the refrigerator and oven, are connected.

Most of the time, walls are painted white. This makes it easier for home owners to add their favorite colors later. This family likes green! ➤

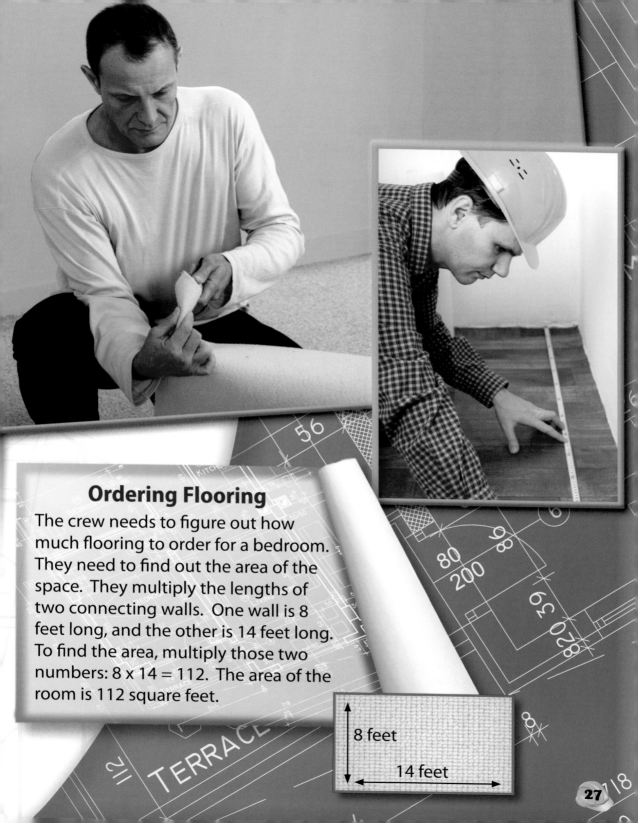

Ordering Flooring

The crew needs to figure out how much flooring to order for a bedroom. They need to find out the area of the space. They multiply the lengths of two connecting walls. One wall is 8 feet long, and the other is 14 feet long. To find the area, multiply those two numbers: 8 x 14 = 112. The area of the room is 112 square feet.

8 feet

14 feet

Landscapers design the lawn and plant trees and shrubs. **Sod** might be laid in the yard. Inside, baseboards are nailed down around doors. Windows and doors are trimmed. Covers are put over the switches and electrical outlets. Knobs are screwed into the cabinets.

An inspector checks the house. He or she lists any problems that need to be fixed before the project is complete.

▼ An inspector checks a house.

▼ A landscaper plants flowers.

A landscaper lays a roll of sod. ➤

▲ A family enjoys their new home.

As you can see, math is an important skill used in home building. It is used at every step in the process—from the first sketch to the last nail that is pounded in.

You also see that it takes many people working together to build a house. But it takes a family to make it a home!

Glossary

appliances—household equipment that run on electricity or gas

architect—a person who designs buildings, houses, bridges, etc.

beams—long, strong pieces of wood or metal used to support floors, ceilings, or roofs

blueprint—a detailed drawing or plan that shows what a house will look like inside and out

budget—the amount of money to be spent for a certain period or purpose

bulldozer—a large machine that is used to clear land

cement—powder made of clay and limestone that becomes hard when water is added

concrete—building material made of cement, sand, gravel, and water

crane—a tall machine that lifts heavy material into place

diameters—the width of circles, spheres, or cylinders

drywall—wall covering pressed between two thick sheets of paper

electricians—people who install or repair electrical equipment

estimate—a careful guess about the amount, size, or worth of something

footings—the groundwork of a building or other structure

foundation—the base on which a house is built

general contractor—a person who contracts others for building construction

geometry—the area of mathematics that studies shapes and objects

insulation—material used to prevent loss of heat

landscapers—people who design what the land around a house will look like

lumber—logs cut into boards or beams for use in building

plywood—strong boards made from thin layers of wood pressed and glued together

property—a piece of land

septic tank—an underground tank that holds waste material

shingles—thin pieces of material placed in overlapping layers, used to cover a roof

sod—a layer of ground with grass

stucco—a material used to cover and decorate walls

surveyor—a person who determines the distances and angles between different points

trusses—triangular structures that form the roof of a house

Index

About the Author

Lisa Greathouse grew up in Brooklyn, N.Y., and graduated from the State University of New York at Albany with a bachelor's degree in English and journalism. She was a reporter, a writer, and an editor for The Associated Press for 10 years, covering news on everything from science and technology to business and politics. She has also been a magazine editor and a writer for education publications and a university website. Today, she works as a writer at the Disneyland Resort, where she oversees an employee magazine. In her spare time, she enjoys visiting Mickey Mouse and riding Space Mountain. She is married with two children and resides in Southern California.

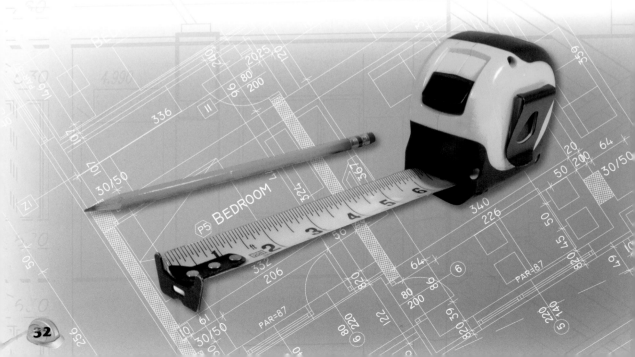